SOME THEY CAN'T CONTAIN

[BY BUDDY WAKEFIELD]

SOME THEY CAN'T CONTAIN [BUDDY WAKEFIELD]

A publication of Write Bloody Publishing, Nashville, TN

For more information or to contact:
buddy@buddywakefield.com

Cover image by Jeff Harmon.
Layout by Nathan Warkentin.

CONTENTS

INTRODUCTION

There is a gnawing desperation evolving from the invasive over-stimulation of media and the high speeds at which prices are being put on passion, humility, integrity and balance. From that desperation flies myriad indigo voices proclaiming that the need felt by government and religion to dictate individuality will not succeed. The greedy heart attack grind of "intelligent" life has claimed so much unfounded power through fear that we have literally allowed infinity to be bent in half, an apparent effort to run in circles, headless chickens on a mission.

As you read this book, thank you for remembering that I am of a gripping and blazing generation of performance poets who have pulled their ribs apart to heave out their voices and give you God, swiftly. We are the fed up grass roots movement of goose flesh, hell bent on living this one life by the way we feel our spines, saying what we mean, refusing to allow the few to preach to the many when it is the many who need to be hearing each other. We are outlaws of the proverbial box determined to expose the shackles of conditional freedom. We are vulnerable with our thoughts and our bodies and we have left the page exponentially bound for the stage to celebrate voice and nuance, body and presence, microphones, flow, people and resonance; to witness the face of a crowd be redeemed, revived and released in the same moment.

Yes there were the Beat poets and, yes, there are hordes more labels of poets who poured a foundation for us, but this book is not for them. This book is dedicated to the stage poets who have taken it to the next level despite intense criticism, who challenge comfort, who vibrate viscerally, and who I've witnessed in 3-minute bursts of verse do more for a mass than Mass ever did for the congregation.

Performance poets like Tara Hardy, Derrick Brown, Michael Cirelli, Jeffrey McDaniel and the artists of Youth Speaks/Brave New Voices will be revered by the next generation of professors and students studying the poets of today, able to detonate the page as competently as they do the stage. These are performance poets who can take hyper-literary page poets up to the school for a spankin' and back again, consistently, but I digress because we do not come without bite.

It is important to me that the reader knows the poems in this book are intended for personal delivery from me to you through the stage. This written compilation of performance poetry is only happening because of the generous folks at The Wordsmith Press in Ann Arbor, MI and Write Bloody Publishing in Nashville, TN, so that those interested alongside myself might have a keepsake. The poems and completed thoughts in this book hold up well enough on the page, but I boast no claim to being a page poet. It's not my aspiration. I would rather the audience see my eyes in person when I get so sure of flight; see my arms swing open like zoo gates to let you in when I know that there is life being pumped through the dilating pores in this room. In anticipation of my being so vulnerable you'll throw stones, I sometimes shake my head like the Bible was literal and I just might burn forever. That's something I can only show you most days, not tell.

There are close and respected friends who've tried to sway me, and I've wanted to be swayed, but more often than not when I pick up a book of poetry I put it down soon. I was not influenced by poets of the page because I don't have that attention. I don't play that instrument. Performance poets and music remain the mediums that excite me, only second to experience. I often wonder whether you will know the intended impact by simply reading my work from a book.

In the fall of 1984 Anchor Bay Entertainment released a movie called *Children of the Corn* while I lived in front of the cornfields near Niagara Falls, New York. This traumatic event – coupled with extensive exposure to Kenny Rogers – is why you will no doubt find me losing a grip often in this book and in my life. If at any point I reveal too much or too little, refer to my disclaimer:

Usually I'm everything, just not today.

With Much Love & Respect,

Buddy Wakefield

. . . .

NOTE: To each and every person of religious conviction and spiritual acceleration reading this infinitesimal book, thank you for your awareness that — despite my sharp tongue and abrasive referrals toward religion — I deeply respect and appreciate your pursuit.

However, if your faith feels like an abusive juvenile corrections facility, or causes you to writhe with guilt to the point of needing medication in any form, or convinces you that there is a god hateful enough to stick you inside a pit of fire forever just because you yearn to be your own savior and your own rapture, then I challenge you to find a god less cruel.

SOME THEY CAN'T CONTAIN

CONVENIENCE STORES [2002]

We both know the smell of a convenience store at 4 a.m.
like the backs of alotta hands.
She sells me trucker crack (Mini-Thins… it's like Vivarin).
She doesn't make me feel awkward about it.
She can tell it's been a long drive and it's only gonna get longer.
Offers me a free cup of coffee, but I never touch the stuff.
Besides, I'm gonna need more speed than that.

We notice each other's smiles immediately.
It's our favorite thing for people to notice
our smiles.
It's all either one of us has to offer.
You can see it in the way our cheeks stretch out like arms
wanting nothing more than to say, "You
are welcome here."

She
shows brittle nicotine teeth with spaces between each one.
Her fingers are bony, there's no rings on'm
and she'd love to get'er nails done someday.
One time she had'er hair fixed.
They took out the grease, made it real big on top
and feathered it.
She likes it like that.
She will never be fully informed on some things
just like I will never understand who really buys Moon Pies
or those rolling, wrinkled, dried-up sausages.
But then again, she's been here a lot longer than me.
She's seen everything
from men who grow dread locks out of their top lips
to children who look like cigarettes.

I give'er my money.

I wait for my change.
But I feel like there's something more happening here.
I feel
like a warm mop bucket and dingy tiles that'll never come clean.
I feel like these freezers cannot be re-stocked often enough.
I feel like trash cans of candy wrappers
with soda pop dripping down the wrong side of the plastic.
I feel like everything just got computerized.
I feel like she was raised to say a *lot* of stupid things about a color.
And I feel like if I were to identify myself as gay
this conversation would stop.

It's what I do.
I feel.
I get scared sometimes.
And I drive.

But in 1 minute and 48 seconds I'm gonna walk outta here with a full tank of gas, a bottle of Mini-Thins and a pint of milk, while there's a woman still trapped behind a formican counter somewhere in North Dakota who says she wants nothing more than to hear my whole story (all 92,775 miles of it).

I can feel it though, y'all, she's heard more opinions and trucker small talk than Santa Claus has made kids happy, so I only find the nerve to tell'er the good parts, that she's the kindest thing to happen since Burlington, VT, and I wanna leave it at that because men — who are not smart — have taken it farther, have cradled her up like a nutcracker and made her feel as warm as a high school education on the dusty back road, or a beer, in a coozy.

I feel like she's been waiting here a *long* time for the one who'll come 2-steppin' through that door on 18 wheels without makin'er feel like it's her job to sweep up the nutshells alone when she's done been cracked again, who won't tempt her to suck the wedding ring off his dick, but will show her — simply — *LOVE.*

She doesn't need me or any other man but she doesn't know that either, and I'm just hopin' like crazy she doesn't think I'm *the one* because the only time I'll ever see North Dakota again is in a Van Morrison song late (LATE) at night, I Promise.

Y'all, I feel like she's 37 years old wearing 51 badly, dying inside (like certain kinds of dances around fires) to speak through you, a forest, if you weren't so taken with *sparks*.
But she was never given those words.
She has not been told she can definitely change the world.
She knows some folks do
but not in convenience stores
and NOT with lottery tickets
so
I finally ask'er what I've been feelin' the entire time I've been standin'
there
still
gettin' scared like I do sometimes
really (REALLY) ready to drive
I ask,
"Is this it for you?

Is this all you'll ever do?"

Her smile
collapsed.

That tightly strapped-in pasty skin
went loose.

Her heart
fell crooked.
She said (not knowin' my real name),
"I can tell, buddy, by the Mini Thins and the way ya drive that

we're both taken with novelty.

We've both believed in *mean* gods.

We both spend our money on things that break too easily like
people.

And I can tell
you think you've had it rough
so especially you should know

it's what I do
I dream.
I get high sometimes.
And I'm gonna roll outta here one day.

I just might not get to drive.

. . . .

In the ridiculously thick June humidity of Huntsville, Texas, when Sam Houston State University's campus resembles most ghost towns, I was there, a Resident Assistant in-training.

I believe it took my employers three years to finally hire me because an R.A. is supposed to be this all-inclusive, really diverse tub of butter with closeted aspirations for becoming a prison guard.

The fact: at this particular point in my journey I was the president of The Christian Cowboys & Friends Fellowship (Christian Cowboys are no different than regular Christians except that they're cowboys... I'm gonna pass on this question), and I was a bull rider. Typically, folks who boast such titles don't get a lot of experience with diversity. I can vouch for that.

I was assigned to live in Kirkley Hall that summer essentially by myself, training and assisting the occasional soccer camp. In fact it was a soccer camp that helped me realize I couldn't blow pot through the bathroom vent without it circulating throughout the rest of Kirkley's four stories.

"There's funny smoke coming from our vent," said Young Soccer Camp.

"Hey, you don't worry about that," I told'm and shut the door.

I was 20.
I knew nothing.
I remember renting The World's Largest Gangbang that summer.
My mother bought me a Hibachi (mini BBQ pit). I used it twice.
I had furniture with hard wood in places my head was supposta rest.
Suzanne Sakowitz brought me a plant named Florence for my birthday.
I gave it to one of the cleaning ladies because my negligence was killing Florence.
The air conditioner allowed roaches to come and go at will.
I developed a twitch because of that creepy shit.
I played guitar a lot back then.
Somewhere in there I wrote Cannonball Man.

Years later it would be my honor and to my utter excitement to perform Cannonball Man as a duet with Tim Sanders of The Seattle Slam scene. He had written the perfect addition to Cannonball Man called Bottle Rocket Slow Motion.

. . . .

NOTE: My mention of Sam Houston State University above is in no way an endorsement or a recommendation. SHSU is literally next door to the prison where Governor George W. Bush signed off on the deaths of 135 individuals without knowing them or reviewing their cases beyond a few minutes each. The guilt of over 40 of those put to death was severely questioned. Aside from the deafening prison energy of the town, SHSU is also one of the "leading" institutions for students of Criminal Justice in the U.S. followed by a densely populated (pun intended) Agriculture Department. Translation: SHSU is comprised of mostly cops & cowboys whose conditioned right wing conservatisms and prejudices run disruptively deep. SHSU's minority students may not see a lot of healthy progress in their pursuit for equality there and seem more likely to develop prejudices of their own, thus losing a grip on what true equality encompasses. If ever in Huntsville, Texas, please find refuge in The Soul Lifters Gospel Choir or History Professor A.C.C. Crimm.

BOTTLE ROCKET SLOW MOTION [1999]

Written and performed by Tim Sanders to precede Cannonball Man at shows.

I am not Genghis Kahn in a feverish state.
I'm not even Genghis Kahn in a wheelchair.

I am not a loaded gun.
I'm useless unless you're performing experiments on the cowardly and inane.

I am the bottle rocket slow motion.
I'm writing this as an excuse to keep the lights on.
I am not writing this to step into the ring with anybody except myself,
and even then
I go down in the second round.

I'm not singing to the stars outside the window.
I'm not at the street corner daring life to take its best shot at me
snatching fireflies from the nighttime and tossin'm down like Boston
Baked Beans.
I'm really not gonna point out to left field to indicate a homerun.

I am lighting fuses for the Cannonball Man.
I am listening to the bam crack calamity boom boom of the typewriter
machine go go go like it's got answers,
like it's not just Oz behind a curtain,
like it's a fully automatic weapon shining at high noon with the clink
clank clink of my spurs outside the saloon.

I can do anything.
I can do *anything...*

CANNONBALL MAN [1994]

On the edge of my seat
at the end of my rope
where riddles bloom
where answers fold
I've got a 20-year story
still to be told
about a cannonball man
in the circus side show.

Now that muther fucker was ready to explode.
He had pressure pourin' in from every hole.
They lit his fuse. They watched him blow
and where he's gonna stop
nobody knows.

'Cause they shot'im off over the cities and the plains
like lilacs - across the sky
like a dove - inside the flames
on a candle wax train to paradise.

But distance - began to spread
between the flight of his feet
and the weight of his head.
And as he curled it all up between his knees
he caught wads of sun breakin' up in the weeds

God, damn, that cannonball man unwound
because to rise then fall is so profound.
The 2000 clowns wanna pile from a car
with a stretcher full of mismatched cannonball parts.

But no, he picked up his brains, his eyes and his teeth.
He gathered his words and he made it all speak.

Then he backed off the show with a well-lit fuse,
stuffed 'imself down in a cannonball tube

      And with a free man's grin he took to flight
      right passed the battling birds in the night
who had cannonball eyes and cannonball teeth
cannonball balls and cannonball wings.
And with cannonballs stuck between their beaks
they all shot down and they broke on the streets.

And as I looked up (with feathers in my eyes)
on the edge of my seat at the end of the line
      I saw lilacs hummin' across the sky
      and a cannonball
      inside the flames
      on a candle wax train to paradise.

*****

Out here
in the distance
in the middle
where I can breathe
from where I see a sign of stunning beings
forming
like clouds
laughing
like water
here
I
will
heal

.

*****

. . . .

Pretend was originally intended to be a group piece based on the line "History is repeating itself in record time," but then I just went ahead and put my spiritual position into words alone. This is my belief system.

PRETEND [2000]

Pretend
on this side
there's an albino monkey
makin' bass in a jug with'is tongue.

Pretend
on this side
there's a pitch black woman
dressed in a slow tornado
who looks so much like the night time she almost turns blue in the sun.
She's gonna carry us through this tune
with Huntsville, Texas and The Soul-Lifters Gospel Choir.
That's my back-up diva.

Pretend
behind me
there's just one
big
bang.

Now it's you.
Pretend you're just bein' yourself.
Pretend you live for a living.
Pretend — inside yer skin — you've got a friend who's willing to give you
everything you ever wanted in exchange for all you've ever been.
Pretend you're more obsessed with this moment
and a little bit less with the way it ends.

And for a moment pretend
this is a plywood lemonade stand with a sign on the front.

It reads:

I've got no more lemons
just my OPINIONS
yours for a DIME-A-DOZEN today
and they'll always be on the table
but only some gonna set ya free.

Now here's where I need ya to believe.
Please.
Believe that here stands a man who pretends not to fall apart
who gets so nervous his lips peel back when we give any slack to the dark side
who gets so god-solid scared yer gonnawannatalkabouttomorrowagain
that he'll pretend to stand and listen
with a sharp look on' is face
while a monkey plays
BASS
BASS
with a back-up diva pullin' back-up faith
for this I-man cross-universe relay race
to try and be more than human
beginning and ending moment by moment
rolled over re-birthing again
because history is repeating itself in record time, y'all,
and we have got to stop actin' like nothin's happening
when we've got 6 billion dawning truths setting 6 billion different suns on you
but we 6 billion gods are still up in arms over what it will cost to follow through
so that YOU can be ME forever my friend
at the same time I get to be YOU
so you can rock me, Brother Rock,
and you can soothe me, Sister Soothe
like one
big
bang.

Because I don't believe the big bang really happened yet.

I think a small bang mighta went
Pfffft!
But the big bang is just on its mark
set
and is really ready to go
kinda like a slow tornado
growin' larger than these 6 billion words
movin' faster than a sky flyin' farther away from every square inch of us
racing birds.
It looks a lot like it would if just one brain in the heart of this place rose up
to the actual size
of the actual voice
it actually contained
into just one head
singing just one song
with a word
and 6 billion looks on its face —

to see a monkey play BASS.
to feel a back-up diva with'er back-up faith
goin' off, y'all

like one
big

bang

NOW *[1997]*

wanna be a monk
wanna be hooked on junk
that makes me
feel for You

wanna live in a stained glass shack
wanna walk with a cross on my back
if that'll get me
closer to You

wanna be pure in heart
wanna tear their talkin' apart
and be quiet now

Just for You

wanna be the meek
wanna walk my caloused feet
on the softest grass
You
ever grew

wanna be of every faith
wanna benefit from every grace
then give it all
back to You

gonna live now
turn these words around
and be entirely
new

Dear Angry **OLDER PEOPLE** *[2 0 0 0]* over 21-ish, anyone who considers themselves an adult, still bitter:

Next time you're wondering what's wrong with kids today, you might wanna check out the examples you've been giving us to work with.

If you ever wanna make sense *of* us then you've gotta make sense *to* us without telling us you're too old to walk that far. You gotta try understanding *why* we like looking like rag dolls, *why* we like looking like the way we feel and *why* we keep our senses floored when it's you behind the wheel.

And if you ever really do wanna understand why we seem so angry, well, for one, you told us we could be anything we wanted to be but right now we're a little busy dodging bombs. Okay and two: rather than celebrating the gifts you've got, we more often see ya blowing fuses over simple mistakes on dinner receipts as if the waitress was purposely ramming you in the ass with dynamite sticks and branding *KICK ME* signs on your faces.

It was an accident. You've got to calm down. Re-think this approach. Ask yourself, "*What...* would Bill Murray do in this situation?"

I've seen fish (hooked) who keep more patience in their worst gill than some of you've got in your best moods. If you were a sandwich at McDonald's they'd call you the *McGrump*. You've *got* to get a grip. Please.

It's been another long day playing games in the schoolyard trying to make sense for an old people who won't be satisfied. So, I suggest ya hush up, turn around, and march those cranky asses straight back to your rooms while me and your sons and daughters try figuring out how to actually use all this forgiveness we found piling up in the laundry you still haven't washed because you've been too busy out prescribing all that hell and giving it away in hand baskets to those who
SEND CASH!   ACT FAST!   CALL NOW!
Well, this is me without my PROZAC!
And this is me just shy of NICOTINE!

And, *muther-FUCKERS*, it's my second time to fail an anger management class, so for the love of greatness, please stop moving the hands of *my* clock to the time *you* had it made. I'm way too busy working out the kinks here. You didn't exactly wind this thing back up when you were through hosing down all the big, bright, violent warning signs we done lit up out in Gangland and on down the road to Columbine where all these kids you can't seem to make any sense of would stop holding you so far off the edge of your seats if you'd start holding your*selves* to the promises you make.

We know you're not perfect
because we're not.
And I know
I ain't perfect.

But I believe I was meant to be.

. . . .

Brian Price and I were yelling things in the parking lot of a shady apartment complex off Garth Road in Baytown, TX. It was some time in the wee hours between 3A.M. and drugs. The sun came up eight or nine times that morning. The words I Got Gone flew out of my mouth there in 1991 as I flailed around like any other self-absorbed teen does when pretending they don't care what you think about them. Proving grounds.

Those are the days that haunt me like good ballads by bad bands, when God was the scariest mutherfucker I ever knew, when Love was conditional. I wrote stacks of notebooks back then like some encyclopedia for the phases of my own fear. I later threw most of them away in an attempt to erase my embarrassment and clear space for writings that would glorify Jesus only. No one could have ever convinced me back then that they really did understand how scared I was, and how normal that is.

I still get terrified when sometimes when no one's watching.

The original opening line in this next piece went something like,
  "I got gone gone gone / tried to come down before the dawn."

The part about throwing my body around like a wand came to me later while I waited in line to see the Sistine Chapel in 1998. I was thinking of this corny ode to Perry Farrell and Tom Waits and Leonard Cohen that went something like:

Me & Tom Waits smoked cigarettes
hunkered down by an un-swabbed city deck
with the ghosts of a Saturday night right by our side

While Perry Farrell something full force in song
he was throwin' his body around like a wand
he traveled in and up and out and something something.

In a ballroom dance with Leonard Cohen
trading skin tight words in perfect form...

That's all I remember, except that later in the piece I tried incorporating Billy Joe Shaver and Roger Waters.

. . . .

My friend, Seth, gets incredibly flustered when there's a yearning in his heart that the tip of his tongue doesn't know how to translate. It makes him ball up inside like a fist. He wants to express himself so badly with words sometimes, but he doesn't always have the catalog of associations at hand to know which words deliver the appropriate expression without losing his cool. In the same way, I can get flush red with anxiety when I want to talk in-depth regarding politics or history. I wish so badly that I had retained historical facts and political jargon to back myself up when expressing how much I despise and wholly distrust George W. Bush. My brain doesn't always turn the trick of accessing facts to back up my intense ill regard for the cattle in mass media's field, especially when I become one of them.

At any rate, I Got Gone has something to do with the little girls who've made my shoes with guns pointed at their heads. This piece I cannot define has something to do with the executives in the logging industry who haven't stepped away from the greed long enough to wrap their minds around a saving grace called hemp; something to do with oil pipelines and Saudi Arabia; something with the people who believe that George W. Bush was elected honorably or was discharged honorably or lives honorably; with 15% of the polar bears on the northern ice cap being hermaphrodites due to PCB's being dumped into the ocean by the same corporations firing the hard workers who made them rich, then moving to Mexico where there won't be a bunch of those annoying U.S. environmentalists to stop them from dumping more PCB's before all of Mexico evolves into an ulcer.

This poem — which will no doubt be shorter than its intro — has something much to do with CIA crack, with Spalding Grey, with Noam Chomsky, with more money spent on wars than on universal healthcare, more money spent on wars than on education, more money spent on wars than on art, or healing. I Got Gone is a reaction to sadists, surcharges, prisons, and laws driven by industry (e.g. Why are you required to wear your seat belt by people who don't really care about you?). I Got Gone has something to do with cops who don't care about anything other than playing god with your life, who pretend to protect and serve, but only take your money and your verbal (or otherwise) submission.

I Got Gone must have something to do with homosexuals being banned from marriage based on sanctity, while there are shows like "Who Wants to Marry A Millionaire" and "Wife Swap" and half of all heterosexual marriages end in divorce. This poem is a civil liberty referring hateful Christians to Matthew 7:4, Bishop Spong, or a joint, so we can stop arguing in circles about it. This poem has everything to do with growing up feeling wrong and guilty, and it's got a shitload to do with drugs.

I GOT GONE [2 0 0 0]

I got gone Gone GONE!
I was throwin' my body around like a wand
and they were yellin',
"Slow down, boy, slow down!"

But I don't get their rigid rules.
They fold their arms out
like a people who praise
while they dawdle in a box between greed and release
as if
this
dawdling speaks for the free
as if
in their praise
they're speakin' for me.

But it's just talk, y'all, and goddamn can they talk
like a people who say they're alive
while they hurdle by on backslides, alibi's, technicalities, loopholes
and a bolt-action judgment.

It's a people in an itty bitty box
who think that just because the top's open now
there'll always be a way to get up and fly out.
And they'll fly out anytime but now.

But *NOW*--
They've got hate-with-a-smile they'd rather expose
so you better be wearin' your expensive clothes in this box
'cause the dark don't just go through their eyes anymore
it shows in the way they bury the poor.
And I don't know who they are,
or what they want,

or where they're comin' from
because their skin's so thick and deep
I can't tell if they've got hearts underneath
from a complete lack
of a rising beat.

So I got gone Gone GONE!
I was throwin' my body around like a wand
and they where yellin',
"Slow down, boy, slow down!"

But I don't get their rigid rules,
yellin' at me,
"Slow down, boy, slow down — wait
No!
Speed up!
Be first! Don't cut!
Get lost! Get found!
Get it right! Learn to fly!
Jump this high! Stay grounded!
Go! Fight! Win!
Shut up! Speak up! Sit still!
Move out!
March!
Stop!"

Am I dizzy God?

"Yeah, you are."

Yeah, that's what I thought
beause from outside the box
lookin' in
I see a people
who've got old guts, old wits,
old thrust and regret

for an old loss on an old goal
that clearly began
this fucked-up caged-in maze no God would ever keep us in.

It's a people who got
bought out, shut down
kicked back and meter read
by an old hope
in an old scene
that we've all been too proud to frame in our bones

so I got gone gone   gone
in a ballroom dance with dusk and dawn
trading skin tight words in perfect form
around an itty bitty box full of people being born,
yellin' at me, screamin',
"Whadaya think you're doin', boy?!"

And I just yelled back, *"Y'all...*
I'm goin' home

for somethin' to ease these fits

so I can drift

lift

instrument

and slow down.

Slow down."

Sometimes
in all the muffled stuff they're talkin'
all that crap

I catch a word or two
just so I'll know what to throw back.
All I wanna do is throw back
to know I'm not alone
and get gone
Gone.

. . . .

"It's been a long time since anyone's called her beautiful
And it's been even longer since she heard she was bright."
— Steven Arrowood

Let it be known that despite suggestions in an old article by *Maxim* magazine, and despite what MTV feeds you through Real Green's *Jackass Countdown*, Steven Arrowood is not only founder of The Dares, but is also king of Grab Ass, The Good Stuff, Blind Thrust Walk and One-Word-Genital-Whips. If you knew him, you'd feel okay about never having met Phil Hartman or Bob Dylan.

You can see one of his most publicized appearances on the aforementioned MTV product. A video called "Don't Wanna Miss A Thing" features Steven with an up & coming ensemble who tentatively go by the name Aerosmith. Steven plays the role of a passionate violinist, possibly with an S.T.D., if I remember right. He's strategically placed far up in the balcony where ya can't really see his face from all the other violinists who got the part. So sly. No stealing the spotlight. That's how his brilliance works.

Those two lines that Steven wrote in the quotes above are borrowed and changed up for my own purposes in this next piece.

A song called "Atmosphere" by Joy Division helped me to fully realize *Fran Varian's Grandmother* after it had been written. Because of that moment with the voice of front man Ian Curtis I saw the invisible escape routes in this poem. It doesn't come to you in words. It comes through thoughts and feelings, and it comes before years of healing, so it begs to be heard carefully.

The work's most obviously repeated lines are also taken with permission. This time, from a work of art called *Yonkers* written by incredible performance poet and friend, Fran Varian.

I wrote *Fran Varian's Grandmother* out of losing faith that there is a reason for everything. I like to believe it's the kind of work that leaves an audience feelin' fast-waked-up from a slow sleep. I fancy it a masterpiece built in the dark by a blind guy, with accents of fractured light bolted to the edges. I just tried to use the word *fancy* in a serious way and made myself giggle.

. . . .

In 1997 I played a dark, miserable acoustic set at a coffeehouse in Huntsville and left the crowd feelin' pretty... gross. I told myself to knock it off with the public self-destruction and humiliation. It's such a lazy intrusive thing to do to yourself and the people who are kind enough to watch you do it without laughing. That was the same night I wrote A Little Ditty Called Happiness.

I retired all my old songs soon after that, but there was a time when I got to feelin' so bad again, and I wrote Fran Varian's Grandmother because of it.

FRAN VARIAN'S GRANDMOTHER [2001]

Fran Varian's grandmother told us she caught a letter from Heaven
saying that the children of her children's generation would be devil's
walking the earth,
and when I hear this – somehow – it feels right.

It feels familiar, like the ghost story about the traveling young couple
who breakdown near a town where a lunatic's on the loose. Boy runs for
help, remember?
Girl hides, covers up on the floorboard.

An hour later there's a single knock on the car top
then another
steady
all night long.

When day breaks
Girl finds Boy
hanging upside down where the wind blows
knockin' his knuckles on the window
and on every dream I had
the night I heard that ghost story.

Her words barge in and outta me now
but I don't know if that's twice a day or once a week
because each time still feels like the first.
"Devil's," she told us, "walking the earth."

When I hear this I can't move and I can't breathe
because it feels so much like ghost stories and bad dreams
makes me desperate to hold the hand of Fran Varian's grandmother
not too hard
not as tight as I'd like to.
I'd keep it calm so I don't seem desperate, but I do

I get so desperate
desperate to know if she caught a second letter
saying *anything*
from *anywhere* up above
that could've mighta maybe mentioned others
not devil's
but others
with halo's shaped like roller coasters you'd stand in line to ride twice.
Others
who don't know how to tell you and still remain humble that
it's been a long time since anyone's called'm beautiful
and it's been even longer since they heard they were bright.

But Franny's grandma doesn't remember catching any other letters
just the one saying that the children of her children's generation
would be devil's walking the earth.

When I hear this, Mom, it hurts
HARD
from my chest
like the dream with the fear
of the man
forever his fatness
all hate
he straddles like whiskers
my stomach
and grins
through my face
the weight of his head so blood red, raked-up, crusted and thick
spit
eyes full-out like a choke hold.
Teeth: split
Ears: twisted
balled-off deaf
now Boy goddamn would ya keep it still!

And I do.
I get scared so still it feels like statues and wind
left in a garden behind some old white house in a dead wheat field
where if *ANYONE* would just yell *MERCY* maybe these lungs could finally fill,
but Fran Varian's grandmother caught a letter from Heaven that said the
children of her children's generation would be devil's walking the earth
and as I gasp and pull for a full breath of air
like air is the only *way out*
her words barge through me again
as if somehow
they're true.

. . . .

There are meetings held by rich people who sit around figuring every possible way to squeeze money out of you. From laundromats to hotels to the fancy new light indicators in cars, you really are subject to their greed in a frequently growing way. They are kudzu and you are a sleeping hiker.

There are scholars of literature (and — more likely — rejected pseudo scholars) who refuse to see the great gap being bridged by the current spoken word movement, enabling students to explore how they love poetry, void of extraneous law and exclusive tradition.

I'm not saying the three groups have anything in common other than their ability to professionally suck soul, like going to a church where the goal is to make you think you are something other than holy. Wholly.

FLARE GUNS AND EARTHQUAKES [2003]

Because it makes a writer appear self righteous
they say to never begin a book or a poem with the word *I*
so I didn't
but you should know

this is about *me.*

If it comes off as self righteous
that's because I speak from a temple
of twenty percent tithing
where too many vandals toting crosses and scandals
have chucked their hymnal pulp so far up into my pit
that I cannot deny it, y'all

I'm fuckin' pissed.

I

I I IIII I I mutherfuckers.

This poem is about me
and some anger
flare guns
and earthquakes
and maybe
I'm gonna yell
but let that stand as a warning
to all the hyper-critical literary poets out there
who have condemned yelling
or even cussing
as a way of *expressing* oneself
through the art of *spoken* word:
I yell sometimes.

If that doesn't fit inside your guidelines
feel free to get up off of your appropriate*NESS*
and fuck off.

I'd be lyin' if I told ya different, y'all
I'm ready to kill somethin'.
I'll probably only get as far as my brain cells
but I'm gonna fuckin' *kill'm.*

My smile is being murdered by the church and the state of surcharges.
The courts in Iowa City recently made me pay them a $250
"self-observation" fee.
I told them I would watch myself for free.
They disagreed.
This is a true story.
Keeping the money dogs at bay is like eating rocks on novacaine.
Soon
I will wail.
My dogs
are barkin.
Rich people
I am one Robin-Hooded dream away from stealin' yer slave trade diamonds
and buyin' me and my crew some loafers and a massage.

Bank of America charges me three dollars
every time I need assistance from a human being
and nearly four dollars when I wanna withdraw my own money
but am outside of my state...
Yeah, I'm outside of my state here!

I've got a voice inside my cell phone telling me how to hang up
when I'm done with my call!
Since the inception of time I have known how to hang up my own phone!
And I have *NEVER* needed to dial *POUND* for more options!
You're wasting my minutes!
Goddamn it!

They can put a man on the moon
but they can't put a voice inside my cell phone
to let me know when I'm about to go over the minutes
on my minute usage plan
just before they start charging me a testicle!
Where red ferns used to grow!
Into giant peaches!
There's your fuckin' poetry quota!

When poets lose their poetry, and their minds
this is the kinda crap yer gonna get
so start payin' my broke ass to write prettier fuckin' images
instead of sandcastles in a colander
if ya really want me to give you what the gods gave me.

This is my job, and I know it's worth more than a car wreck in a movie.
A car wreck in a movie could pay off my financial aid
fill the holes in my teeth
fix the opaque spots in my vision
and have enough left over for some groceries and a
gotdamned bottle of Xanax!

But instead
my stomach works as a 24-hour meat grinder
fueled by butterflies and college debts that have since dominoed
into eight different papers named Bill
who come over and trash my apartment once a month with treaded water.

And, yes, I *know* it was inappropriate to have used the word *poet* or *poetry*
in a *poem*
Professor
but *it's a little too late for that now!*

Last week I went to church for the first time this side of freedom.
I was hoping to give back the baggage they gave me in exchange for all
the tithing

[39]

but no one was there.
Instead, it was a letter stapled to the door from the preacher
said, "My parishioners now work for the state, and I, the preacher, am
out being filled with the words of the National Poetry Slam."

Y'all, there is an entire congregation who go by the exact same name
live inside my ears when I'm angry and alone and writing.
If you stood us side by side to a Bible
we'd be the ones who looked blessed.
Broke
but blessed.
Without the proper fork
minus the etiquette
and one late payment away from a pawn shop
but blessed.

This poem may have meant nothing to you
but I am confident that tonight
my taking the time to actually write out my anger
instead of acting on it
has saved the life of at least eleven people in parking enforcement.

I mutherfuckers.
This flawless poem was about me
and some anger
flare guns and earthquakes
and maybe
you.

. . . .

Some They Can't Contain is most sentimental to me. For one, because I wrote it in a time when I wasn't sure if it was okay to say things like "bees on flowers with honey on hold" and "screaming, sparkling Gods." Those are feminine, ya know?

Two, because it contains lyrics from the first full song I ever wrote in tenth grade called *Another Someday* whose original rhythm was blatantly stolen from a song by a band called Skrew who I heard by way of Bret Turner who is the only man on earth who can play its original version in full on the guitar and enjoys it for the death metal ballad it really is.

And three, because of the line *I drop my jaw at fire when it's flyin' out my eyes.* I liked that line so much I wrote it on the wall above my bed with glow-in-the-dark goo. It was all smeared and nuts. I've since moved from that place. I forgot to wash it off the wall before I left. It would have been fun to see the look in the new tenant's eyes first time she woke up from a dream and *I drop my jaw at fire when it's flyin' out my eyes* was glowing above her face.

Some They Can't Contain used lines from five other things I'd written since 1989. I remember listening to Jon Spencer Blues Explosion's "Make It Alright" while putting together the Slam version of *Some They Can't Contain*. The version herein has the beginning tacked on, as it is on the CD *A Stretch of Presence*.

Years after writing this completed version I sat listening to Pink Floyd and realized I had ripped off a line from them too back in the day. Tenth grade... That was a long time ago. I've subtly changed the line about radiating glass to make it mine, but there's no denying how most of my work somehow displays influence from the incredible artists who shaped and continue to fine tune my own writing.

SOME THEY CAN'T CONTAIN [1998]

Leave your resident flesh.
Bring on your boogie man.
You're gonna know what's on the road.

Underneath all that skin
there's someone louder than
the literal zoo you've come to know.

Ah do ya got butterflies'
nervous infusion
could it all be one huge illusion?
Maybe that's something
we'll never know.

But I'll go.

I'll go with you on your broken sleigh
until your eyes finally receive the day
and I'll call
till you call back to me
      back to me

                                             back to me

              back to me

back to me
back

because I drop my jaw at fire when it's flyin' out my eyes
and I plunge my coiling wires in the water till I rise
above frogs
and pop rocks
and boxes

of roof tops
and the noises
I can't outrun
even when I'm running twice the speed of sound already
and three times the speed of my blood

'cause everybody's got voices

and everybody's got some they can't contain

like my need to be redeemed
at any time
in any place
where I see my Jonathan Seagull
being tattooed on the fists
of men who fear we'll think what we think
about the laws *they* can't resist.

So you can bring on your boogie man
loading his fuss
and gunning his fattening desire
'cause I've got bees
on flowers
with honey on hold
for those made of gold but wrapped in wires
who keep themselves inspired by the way they feel their spines
screamin, sparkling gods who gotta live by the way they shine.
And this is not a dot-to-dot plot
or a battle on *your* god
of the makers of money and the odd mockers of drum
who all peel and staple great gobs of Marge Maple
the girl they just gotta slum.

No, this is my time and place.
This is me saving my saved face.
So if my heart starts to radiate

bold, broken glass
man, relax
it always pumps this fast

because I drop my jaw at fire when it's flyin' out my eyes
and I plunge my coiling wires in the water till I rise.

. . . .

Aside from the deletion of two small paragraphs to protect the innocent, the following self-loathing crap is an unedited journal entry. This entry — coupled with a true occurrence at a grocery store in Wallingford (Seattle, WA) — is the reason for the performance poem Aaron. Some of the word choices and delivery are heavily inspired by George McKibbens of Brooklyn and Claudia Sherman of Long Beach.

January 30, 2003
Schindler

It's 12:22a.m. in Marshall, TX. My Aunt Tina sleeps upstairs after burying her husband of 25 years today. She'll wake up in 2 hours and 27 minutes to take me to the airport in the city where I was born. Shreveport, LA. I'm in her cabin a quarter mile off a road that is 1 mile off the main road 10 miles from town. Everyone else has left. Every surviving member of my family was piled inside here today (including the longest mullet I've ever witnessed which is officially and proudly a part of my family)...

...I just watched Schindler's list for the first time, and I thought of spiritual...angles. The one about how we chose to be who we are. Each time we die we come back in a different body with attributes we chose. I don't know if it's true; I just hope that if it is, I hope I'm done this time. I don't wanna come back here anymore. I don't like it here. I hope I was already Jewish and black and enslaved. I hope I was burned alive. I hope I was already wrongfully accused and beaten badly. I hope I was German and hateful and rich once. I hope I was a woman loved entirely by her man. I hope I was a hero and a thief and skinny. I hope I've already been retarded and already seen my family succeed, each one. I hope I was the governor and prisoner and each animal I was supposed to be. I hope like crazy I already got to be a monk and that I once breathed steady for an entire lifetime. I hope I was already a famous artist, maybe without an ear. I hope I already knew how to fly a plane or invented something profound, and that I've already been a dedicated athlete. I hope I was hungry once from the time I was born til the moment I died and maybe came back as a king who hated everyone and killed them for fun until the day I died at a miserable old age, and that I came back with a message, and a plague, and a cure. I hope I was Schindler more than anything else, or William Lloyd Garrison, or the guy who colored-in cartoons before computers. Either way, I hope this is it. I hope I'm done. I don't wanna come back. I really don't like it here. From the ulcer on my tongue to the work waiting for me in Oakland tomorrow night. From the fat on my gut to the smoke that fills this house even when no one's smoking. From the obvious answer, to the men who

• •

hide it with all their might. From the rude & cynical & cruel to the fake & insecure & my own lack of integrity. I sit here in this dramatic onslaught of myself and walk in circles wondering why it is I stay, even now, as I sound like my high school journal and contradicting my newest piece about moving forward. The only reason I can find is for love. I really wanna share in a true mutual love. I wanna learn how to receive love. And to have a child. Love's just gotta be worth living for if I wanna bring a child here to experience it.

This life is so profound that I find myself merely writing about it. I've yet to help build a skyscraper, or help feed the homeless anything worth duration. I drive in a car. I perform poems. I see Schindler's List and I fall so silent that I must write before I scream. I am ceaseless in wearing myself out with good intentions. I give myself credit, then deny it simultaneously. I relax and feel uncomfortable in such an overlapping motion that I stay restless. I I I I I I. I NEED Love so I can get over myself...again.

Unedited. Shower, then fly all day. Work tomorrow, then drive, then perform, then endure til I can get home in August where I will stablize and keep my heart open for loving like I can't get hurt, even though I know I can. Buddy

AARON [2003]

He's got a two-year-old in his left arm being terribly two.
His wife is nagging relentlessly.
I know his name is Aaron
because she begins and ends most every sentence with his name.
I also know that it's spelled A – A – R – O – N
because I can hear the extra A in the dental drill of her voice.
She sends my nerves off to war.

The fourth swipe of the food card fails.
This time Aaron puts back the orange juice.
There goes breakfast, again, and the red on Aaron's face
grows one shade closer to crying.

Though you may feel for him now
I am positive you wouldn't like Aaron
unless the two of you met at a hot rod show
sponsored by Hooters, bad breath, crystal meth, then NRA
and *you*
were somehow havin' a good time.

Aaron has offended everyone he's ever met
but right now
as he tries to break free from check stand #6 with all his might
I can tell Aaron wants everyone to know
he's sorry.

"Aaron, this is why we're on food stamps, because you can't count, Aaron."
She growls at him as if she were being paid good money to do so.
I know he's thought of killing her (or himself) at least twice this week already.
Today, it's Monday, and as much as I'd love to believe differently
as much as I desperately wish to hug him and tell him he will soon see the Light
I don't think Aaron is gonna get out of this life what he came here for.
Not this time around.

His two-year-old son bats him in the face
and squirms like a spiral
screaming
downward.

Now, follow me here.
One more time.
From the top.
With Feeling.

I hope I've already been an ape at every stage of evolution.
I hope I've already been a beautiful woman of color
made to feel ugly for wearing that skin
by men who claimed to be Christian with a straight face.
I hope I've already been every evil element in the dark half of this whole
spectrum
that each one of us has already met on terms as bad as Nazi & Jew
rich and poor
the United States and East Timor
that — somehow — this is the moment we all make good.
And I hope with all my heart
you'll give me one more minute to come full circle
because even if you don't
I will not let up until I take it all the way around this time.

I hope I invented a drum,
set a world record,
sculpted birds,
built a skyscraper, a lake, a crop circle and a home.
Hope I danced with my tribe around fire
(on peyote, near the tide).
Y'all, I hope I lived at least one lifetime
wherein I did not love buttery pastries *so much*
or that, even if I did,
I had a really high metabolism.

But the only lives I'm absolutely sure I lived are these:

Once, I was a child
who never felt complete about holding anything until it was broken,
who got erections from the smell of gasoline,
and who threw food on the floor bought with the six dollars
given to his mother by a pawn shop in exchange for her high school ring.

In the very next life, I was a teenager
who never felt complete about anyone holding him unless they were
broken too,
who got erections from the smell of suicide,
and who was kicked out of class for refusing the Pledge of Allegiance.

Then one day, for an entire lifetime, I was Aaron
without enough left in me to get what I came here shoppin' for.

"Aaron! You're holding up the whole line, Aaron!"

"I DON'T FUCKIN' CARE ABOUT THE WHOLE LINE!"
He tells her, and seeing how I am next in line
he makes certain I hear this.

I, startled,
realizing who I am
and how far I've come
with the hope that this is my very last time around
say back to him, "Aaron, my friend, *maybe*
maybe that's the difference between you and me."

. . . .

There's a live performance of Marbles in the Trees hidden at the end of track 24 on my first CD A Stretch of Presence. The piece preceding it on that same track is a live spoken word version of A Little Ditty Called Happiness. It was recorded while opening for The Pink Chihuahuas in 1999 at The OK Hotel in Seattle. That amazing all-woman punk band was responsible for my first gigs outside of Slam. I had been on stage for poetry maybe five times before Annie LaGanga, the lead singer, invited me out to do a couple pieces before they took the stage. Pink Chihuahuas would always play with Cringe, this aggressive group of speed freaks who you'd think were just shy of slitting your throat if they weren't such overtly friendly guys. It was punk shows. I would throw on this persona like Wesley Willis was bangin' Tom Waits and — in the spirit of Geoff Trenchard — I would just fuckin' dive man.

The actual studio track of A Little Ditty Called Happiness was recorded in Joe Kowalke's closet in Castro Valley, CA while I wore a bright orange robe and a wig and glasses that made me look like Elton John, backwards. None of anything I've mentioned thus far has anything to do with the next piece though.

I read Marbles in the Trees to my mom as soon as I finished writing it in Pearland, TX circa 1998. I'm glad I've grown out of that phase where I feel the need to rattle off my latest poem to the first person whose attention I can steal. When I was done reading it Mom said, "I like it... it's more your kind of thing."

Murder in the Red Barn by Tom Waits had a lot to do with me writing Marbles in the Trees.

MARBLE'S IN THE TREES [1998]

Y'all come around.
Come on now.
Pay no mind to the fumes.
I got somethin' to say about the folks doin' time in this room.
Ya see the walls' they been whistlin' downright fattenin' yella-bellied tunes.
Check the mirrors for yer orders.
Grab a seat in the blues.
Yer waitress, she'll be with ya soon as she tends to her perfume.

Annie!?

Now that's one chicken, no head.
One backbone, loose.
One musclebound contraption with a fool's gold tooth.
But the broiler's frozen down
so you gonna hafta take it raw
and excuse the dishes
they wouldn't fit in our sink full of dirty thoughts.

Hey, Dingy Grin, how you been?
I see there's thoughts in yer lap
and yer killin' that tobacco while it's killin' you back.
Nah, now it's good to know yer totin' those excuses in yer sack
'cause you gonna need'm
if we bring back yer past.

And you, what's yer name? Why the wait? Make a choice.
We can serve it on the rocks or we can spike it with a voice.
But if you ain't hungry or thirsty then you gotta stop makin' noise
'cause I best be fixin' orders for the starvinest girls and boys.

See, y'all, we could be outside

playin' marbles in the trees
watchin' a spotless future move us
jigglin' fireflies in the breeze.
But no here we go again mouth agape a-waitin' for someone free
to feed us what we want when what we got is all we need.
Y'all we ain't all that hungry, just a dash misled.
How 'bout I have that waitress bring some somethin' to keep yer heads?

Annie!?!

ORDER UP! We got a mountain! A mountain of somethin' right.
The menu's callin' it Fruit, but you might say it's the Light
and it's only good for now, right NOW
(the greatest item of all we price)
'cause you know that time is money
and this one'll cost ya life.

But the taste lasts forever and it's served with a sturdy spine,
a side of greens and smiles and a chilled piece of mind
a slice of life, toasted lightly, then buttered on a side
and a jug of lime to chase the bite in our famous recycled pride.

So you better get it while it's hot
or you can wait until ya freeze
but I'm-a be out back
playin' marbles in the trees.

A MOMENT

I mean like a fuckin' fountain.
Maybe not a marble masterpiece
but a wide, chipped-tooth, built like a brick shithouse, cracked
cement cannon of a fountain
reaching up through the center of a city
like a picture, flooding,
the pressure proportionate to passion at its purest.
It's the tree that despite falling in a forest
with no one around for miles
breaking its thick oak bark in tight bundles twisting from the bottom
can still be heard quite clearly by every ear in the world
as it turns to timber and shouts
"I ain't goin' down without makin' noise!"

(I wrote that after Michael Moore's Academy Award speech.)

WORRIED MOTHER HAIKU

Mom reminds me of
Windshield wipers on high speed
During light sprinkle

THOUGHTS I HAVEN'T FINISHED THANKING

Guy walks into a bar.
Takes two sips.
Walks out.

Bedrooms and battlescars
both keep well in the dark.
Hard dark.
Paid with uppercut and heart spark
spark plugs and fist
first
release.

I talk too much. If you see me being quiet, don't ask me what's wrong.
I'm just practicing.

I know a woman with cataplexy whose body shuts down (in the same way
a narcoleptic suddenly gives out) every time she is overwhelmed by an
emotion. I wonder how she will fall in love.

Gandhi's autobiography is on my pillow.
I put it there every day after making my bed
so that I'll remember to read it before falling asleep.
I've been reading it for six years.
I'm on chapter two.

I call my balls "my boys" sometimes
And I still think it's funny.
There are things I wish I wasn't so comfortable telling you.

Everything is out there.
It's why they call it "everything."

The first time my town saw the sky
it sucker-punched us in the throat
left us breathless
said, "I'm gonna keep you awake some nights
without touching you.
You'll make it up, the pain,
you always do."
Now my town only buys drowsy formula sky.

You look good in your tidal wave
toe-to-toe with the mean blue moon
head raised up like a light house.
You are buttercups spraying out the mouths of doves
fireworks stuck in the air.
You're a freestanding landing pad
held together by choir claps.

FOR GOODNESS SAKE

There is one plant able to provide:

1) PAPER without killing trees
2) FUEL for cars, buses and trucks without the harmful sulfide emissions
3) ALL OF OUR ENERGY on just 6% of our farm land
4) PAINTS & VARNISHES with no toxic fumes or residues
5) BIODEGRADABLE PLASTICS
6) MEDICINE for glaucoma, asthma, migraines, AIDS, cancer, arthritis, emphysema, anorexia, stress, cramps, epilepsy AND
7) FOOD for people, animals and birds?

The plant is called hemp, and it would drastically help eliminate the constant environmental dilemmas we face in our global community. Hemp is currently illegal on the basis of government-imposed stigma and corporations who might not reap financially from the necessary change.

There's been a HUGE mistake. Turns out that, aside from folks who choose to inhale smoke and damaging their lungs, hemp is absolutely harmless. How much longer are we gonna passively watch ignorance dominate and fester in this arena? STEP UP.

The Hemp Revolution (VHS/DVD) is highly informative as well as entertaining.

Also, buy responsibly. Go to www.knowmore.org and type in the name of any corporation to find out the good, the bad and the ugly regarding the business practices (e.g. environmental impact, human rights, political influence). Ya might wanna think about not supporting corporations who work to work you over. Think maybe positive forward progress might happen if they're not the ones in charge anymore? Apathetic? Or doing your part?

If I may use a wording I learned from Jared Paul when he stood up at

the end of a show to compliment the vibe at The Seattle Slam, "I would
be remised if I didn't take this opportunity to say so."

. . . .

Voices was highly influenced by a band named Lincoln with a song named *Blow*.

Voices uses lyrics from 4 songs I hadn't finished, 2 that were never mine in the first place (thanks to The Kinks and 4 Non Blondes), and 1 allusion to a rumor which may or may not be true.

Voices contains some of the most accomplished and talented air guitar writing in years (don't mean to toot my own horn). Its composition was influenced by several days that were dead set on throwin' down with me.

Voices breathes an ohm for the angry.

Voices is a great way to break up a spoken word set and gives me something fresh to do on stage.

NOTE: At a performance in Vancouver, British Columbia I was told that the beaver is a prominent Canadian symbol. My use of the beaver in this piece has nothing to do with promi-nence or Canada. It may, however, be construed as a symbol.

VOICES *[2000]*

(air chords = A/E/D)

There were voices
I was tryin' to shake
so my million monkeys typin' up rules could break
away
from station K-Hey-U-Ahw-Feel-For-Me.

And there were hound dogs barkin' like a mile away
There were June bugs beggin' for the rights to May
And I was thinkin'...

...Sorry, I was thinkin' —

We oughtta rrroust our bums in double-wide circles
say fun words like *birbble* or *gerbils*
but that's not to imply that rousting our bums
has anything to do with gerbils
at all.

And we can bake past times up in a cloud-shaped dish
spike that batter with yellow bricks
pop spit bubbles in betwixt our lips
and pull the bible belt back
through the loops it missed.

And say hey yea yea yeah yeah
hey yea yeah
I said hey...
What uh...
what's goin' on...

with these voices
I been tryin' to shake
like a micro hula hoop hoopin' a grape?
Yeah it's a mixed-up jumbled-up macro grape
in my hooola.
Uh uh oh my hooola.
H-U-L-A, hooola.
Hula-hoopin' up moods on the hips of a dove
who wears a prosthetic wing that fits like a glove
to fly bi-polar bears round trip for free
with first class seating for
everything.

But it's like bird chirps makin' a move on the screams
of a beaver brought down by a kingdom of false teeth
a beaver wood-chuckin' out a method of feeling

a beaver named Lincoln with logs for me
so proud of his stick-chipped quick-witted grin
weasel up-poppin' from the child within
who builds better toys in a moment than
he can for a moment that builds to an end.

(air guitar solo)

He's here to make toll roads all charge paper machet
pull his point from stacks of hay
and finger paint phones for the call of the wild
like the wild still had a say!

Hey hey!

So we can bake past times up in a cloud-shaped dish
spike that batter with our yellow bricks
pop spit bubbles in betwixt our lips,
and pull the bible belt back
through the loops it missed

And say
hey yea yea yeah yeah
hey yea yeah
I said *HEY?!*
Whu-

What's goin' on?

. . . .

All the Time is another guitar song whose lyrics I still enjoy singing once in a while.

All the Time was most influenced by Leonard Cohen.
I wrote it the same week as Marbles in the Trees.
I sent them both to Leonard Cohen.

Leonard is clearly experiencing delays with his postal service because I have still not heard back from him. I sent him a postcard from Seville, Spain once. He didn't respond to that either. Attempt after attempt and even still Leonard has not contacted me. All the operators claim my phone line is working fine. I'm confused, Leonard, and I worry.
I will try to reach you again tomorrow.

Monks are so totally unpredictable. I hope he's alright.

Leonard, if you're reading this, seriously, dude, digits (206) 226-5708.

ALL THE TIME *[1 9 9 8]*

If I had a dime
for every wise man who lost his wise mind
I'd be willing to buy
the very first time they saw the Light

'cause I forget the stages of numb
when I go to where they're comin' from
and I forget what tune I was told to hum
yet it's right here all the time.

and if I had a dime
for every gunslinger's gold-diggin' plight
I might be willing to buy
a bullet for each one into the light

'cause I forget the stages of numb
but I know'm when I see'm comin' one by one
and I forget which tune I was told to hum
when I remember how to fly
high
right here all the time
yeah
unless I leave to use my eyes
I'm right here all the time.

Right here.
All the time.

And you're right there toyin' with love
by the looks of that oiled-up rubber glove
and I'd be willing to bet
you don't know how good it gets

'cause you've become the stages of numb
so busy beatin' yerself with yer tongue
and you forget what tune you were told to hum
but you been hummin' it all the time

yeah
right here all the time
unless I leave to use my eyes
I'm right here all the time.

Right here.
All the time.

. . . .

Arizona Summers was written on a tour pass through Mesa, AZ. My love for the poets and organizers of Mesa is lasting. They have rescued and revived me twice after burglaries on tour and they have always saved a place for me in their home. After a year and a half of touring, writing very little, I finally sat down and wrote this piece for the Arizona poets and Mesa. I would also like to dedicate this to Houston, TX, Shreveport, LA, Memphis, TN and Singapore.

NOTE: My car has no air conditioning.

ARIZONA SUMMERS *[2 0 0 2]*

The day broke over my face like a moist ass.

Lucky for me though
Arizona lines all its strip malls with little pipes
that emit mist
so I can stay cool
because *that* works.

Don't get me wrong. I ain't complainin'.
I mean how awesome is it to sweat so much you don't even hafta buy water?
All ya really gotta do is take off yer shirt and wring yer body weight out
into your mouth, then yer good for like, what, ten more steps before the
sun beats ya down into so much melted tar...
Bad ass.

Hey, anybody got a curling iron I can rub up along my skin?
It's just that I'm not quite fuckin' hot enough here in Arizona.

Oh yeah, and I've got a new trick (that I can only do in Arizona)
where I take off my shoes on the sidewalk and look like a candle
being melted
from the bottom up.
I'd do it for ya now but I can only pull it off once
like a bee sting
then I *die.*

Really though, who among us doesn't love to feel like we live in a blow torch?

Listen, if you're from Arizona
I'm not making fun of your home.
I'm making fun of *you*
for gathering there
and building a community

in an oven.
Smooov move.

Hey anybody got a lighter?
Oh wait, *nevermind*
I'll use my forehead!

Ya know what would be really awesome
is if it could get any more uncomfortably fuckin' hot in here
like maybe we could all fart at once
or wear a collective turtle neck?

I'm gonna pretend I didn't see a dead dog on the roadside today, bubbling.
And I'm gonna pretend that the road it was on wasn't bubbling as well.
And that the thermometer in my black car
in the high heat of mid-afternoon didn't actually say,
"goddamnit!"

Y'all, there's only one reason to live in Arizona.
It's if you're a reptile.
But forgimme
I forget how cozy reptiles can be
like cactus
or sand.

All the more reason to move to Arizona
a land of many choices...
Let's see, do I wanna stay inside today?...
Or DIE!

I dunno
but I have to go now.
The underside of my balls just turned into a waterfall
and my sponge is broken.

. . . .

Thin Ice was written out of an overwhelming need to lock a permanent hug around my artistic roots when I found myself writing too much for the crowd and not exploring my own catharsis enough. I have stumbled upon an understanding that in order to even approach being a brilliant artist one has — in some way — got to make his/herself vulnerable. Truly vulnerable.

I brawled with myself over whether or not to publish *Thin Ice* for several days. There are a lot of people I don't want to read this poem. It is not my goal to shame anyone, but I feel like there are a few who will no doubt read *Thin Ice* and be ashamed of, or even embarrassed for me. As a spoken word artist for a living I've had a habit of revealing too much about myself unnecessarily.

The final decision to publish this poem comes in honor of all the lyricists and writers and painters who made it okay to be a deviant child dancing, who gave me permission to love my entire self and skulls and black, scuffed tongues and hearts swollen, who reminded me as a twelve-year-old and a teenager that I was not alone in this sometimes terrorizing human experience where anyone can be made wrong for anything. This poem is in honor of those artists who've exposed themselves before their peers and continue to do so, expanding the constricting comfort zone that has for far too long plagued dialogue in our homes.

This poem is for the nomad, the nervous, the hunter, the zoo, and for the catalyst of the instrument I played to get to you. It's for the bastard, his father, for the porcelain doll, and to the critic racing here for the words to write me off as I sing for the grinning, for the bearing, and for the sprawled out into rage, and for their desperate amendments to keep my heroes out of range when I write it for the eggshells you're walkin' on, and to the circlin' ya do, and to the slow-approach-me, anything goes, gear up to be amused in a poem for the marching, for the watching, debating the dream, so buttered-up and thirsty, imploding from the steam.

This poem is for me, and for the minority it may reach.

If just one starfish out there gets thrown back because of this poem then my work is right.

I own it.

"I have had the wind knocked out of me, but never the hurricane."
-- Jeffrey McDaniel

THIN ICE [2 0 0 3]

There is a fear so paralyzing it gets to be called *insanity*
a word misused as often as *love.*
I know
because I was raised by unequal parts of both.
Both were unconditional
with loopholes
you know
for the conditioning.

My life was built inside a straw mansion of these contradictions.
So was yours.
But I can confidently promise
you don't want this poem to be about you.

I have been a children's book composed of pornographic clippings
wadded up
stuck with a stick
dipped into space
then watched
awkwardly.

I've been a rock slung shot from a boomerang
off the edge of a fine line that
keeps dividing eggshells
from concrete
without telling me.
Most times I have no idea where I stand with you.

I have been a blurred blue light reclined
stretched out on an airplane seat
pretending there was no machine
no passengers
no baggage

realizing only that
this is what I would look like
flying through the sky alone.

But gravity
it keeps winning.
So I'm gonna come clean now.

I
am a terrified sexual deviant
who runs the risk of dying
without ever having shared
in a true mutual love.

It's why I keep elbow thorns
thick and to the point
better than the kind demons get to wear
but heavier.

And there's jungle gyms bolted to the palms of my feet.
They tremble each time I lay a new card on the table.

As for the tears I keep tears for a face
I've learned how to break'm down
with the tips of my smile for fun

I have a strength so strong
I can crush myself.

And despite the constant shifting focus
this will
in the end
all make sense.
I promise.

That's what I love about God

someone to take the pressure off
of these cinder blocks
fastened with elastic straps
stretched back from my chest
released
and on impact
reloaded.

I have been winded by the locomotive fear
riding back and forth across the tracks
of my sliding closet door
letting out only one secret at a time
so as not to run my friends and family over
with disappointment.

And here's the disappointment this time...

In the seventh grade Jimmy told me
if I didn't give him fifty cents a day
he would beat me up.

At least once a week I would miss payment
on purpose
but Jimmy never beat me up.

His integrity and business-sense as a bully
were very bad.

By the eighth grade
I was forcing Jimmy to take my fifty cents.
It's the only way I knew how to keep his attention.

Listen, the fear was never Jimmy.
The fear was of anyone finding out
I was giving that guy fifty cents a day
for sex I'd never get to have

less the mind-fuck
in my bedroom
after school.

Yes Captain Obvious
I know this is fucked up
but the whole event was as innocent
as the one time you went rubbin' yourself up against that bed post
when ya thought no one was lookin'.

So if we could all rephrase the question
from
"What was your most embarrassing moment?"
to
"What was your most embarrassing year?"
then
I *might* be able to give you an honest answer
instead of feeling like a million monkeys typing
faster than any of us can talk and
swingin' pound for pound with the ghosts
and voices telling me
I am not allowed to write my own way out
of someone else's holy book
when the truth is
I am a perfect part
of the exact point
at which *all* individual human beings meet
and the spectrum of voices
weaving themselves in between and screaming
every sick thought you've ever had
and every twisted feeling you've ever felt
are what make this painting
complete.

I
am a third generation catatonic

given just enough willpower
to watch you and your god deny me
without laughing
like
crazy.

These skates?

They were made for thin ice.

. . . .

The fact that I have the friends I have is proof I've done something profoundly right with my life. Moving Forward is not only for them, but also dedicated to one of the most talented female writers in performance poetry, Barbara Adler, who gave me the confidence to perform this piece correctly.

MOVING FORWARD [2002-?]

If you think being dysfuncted and damaged, strapped to your baggage, dirty, ruined and hurt like critical, cynical, scathing, if you're lost or have come up missing, scarred and scared (or pretending you aren't), when you think that's all you've got, it's not. The sadness you wear around like a trophy is intriguing at most, but it's miserable, and about as original as a frat boy with a visor cap. So step up.

I'm not tryin' to motivational speech ya
or leave out all your excuses for hating so hard.
I'm just givin' you good information.
Don't tell me I don't understand.
I was feeding my anger and depression twelve-step meals twenty-four-seven
before your balls were the size of a corn nut.
Go ahead.

Go down that spiral again.
But you need to know I ain't goin' back in there
because each time
feels like I'm being hogtied and hassled by a massive pack of wolves who stalk children till they finally crack from the impact of a lack of backbone and tact, hit hard by the fact that they're part of the lab testing one-track maze rat tricky traps, mind-mapped onto stacks of kid-you-are-really-unwelcome-here mats made by fat cat wolf packs, sharp as tacks, leading manic depressive fractured hands convinced by a dick in the system's pants that we won't amount to jack. Jack, if they catch you goin' down on that gap, buyin' into that martyr-on-a-meat-rack crap, on purpose, nervous, feelin' worthless and killed before you even tried cutting the straps...

whole food chain's gonna laugh
just before you go unnoticed.

So pull out the slack.

I know it sucks.
That's why I won't go back in there, with or without you.
Forget about it.

It only gives ya wall-to-wall numbing under both yer feet and backstab wounds on both yer cheeks from the turning them and running away from the child you have not set free from the people who let you down by the way they refuse to recede through a distance you've already cancelled out with a pulse that holds you still now on feet afraid to run while you're runnin' as fast as you can possibly run.

And the further you move through the grooves of the words of that hyped up and hateful god you don't trust, the louder it makes me shout. I swear to that same god who man created in his own image that I'd shout my nuts out to help you walk away from this, but I will never *ever* go back in there. I refuse. And I know we're missing some pieces to the puzzle you possibly didn't choose, but just bring me what ya got, come, meet me in the middle. Run. Run river run flow, flow eyes flow. Do not die in the way you will not let go of that fully automatic intent to grow into perfect perfect perfect.

Stop. Stay here tonight. We can compare imperfections by light, swap battle scars and faults for flight, have a massive aggressive ingestion of night. I will do anything you want me to from this side of the fine line, but I will not bunch myself together like a coven of uncomfortably dressed gothic children and bow down to the fear of never coming out ahead, on top, in step with the rhythm of my own concepts, dancing.

So if I seem just a little bit cocky or a lot too unafraid it's because I know I will not go back in there and hide my life away. It makes my water train turn to steam. It makes being amazing seem sick and obscene. It pulls hope (like a rope) from my heart through the holes in my throat, misplaces me pace with irregular notes and beats stopped up by the blood running backwards from a future choked off by the knots in my knees after a lifetime of begging somebody else's God to ease up and let me breathe. It happens every time I come between the downward spiral and its upward dream. Man I done been through too many valleys at midnight to let that happen again to me.

I know you're lost, and I know when you feel so alone and so far gone you'll try to convince anyone who'll buy it that no one understands the times you don't believe in yourself or the reasons you won't belong. But there are beaming rows of undertones *released* showin' off every black rainbow twistin' up outta yer back (looks like angels done fucked up some railroad track and stacked'm out like wings). You're beautiful dressed up in the steel and speed. But you keep acting like hiding in that closet's gonna somehow set ya free.
Not true.
I've seen your chest explode each time your smile retracts. In fact, I've watched you watching dancing children dying not to laugh with everything out loud because your spines caught up on the downward slack of spirals spinning out.

So please, put down those powerful works of art you've been carvin' on your skin with knives in the dark and just *know* that somebody heard you scream
for Love.

If you think being jealous and overwhelmed and beaten and tired, dysfuncted and damaged, strapped to your baggage, dirty, ruined and hurt like critical, cynical, scathing, if you're lost or have come up missing, scarred and scared (or pretending you aren't), when you think that's all you've got, it's not.

I watched you ring a bell once, all day long, because you thought it gave angels wings able to link up like children hands. It's no secret when you do these things.
It's no secret that you live for the chance to come clean and be redeemed.

Here's your chance.

There are no angels who have any more power than you do.

If you're gonna stay there in the thicky tar of it,
feathers ruffled and stuck to the scorch, then maybe you're right.
Maybe I don't understand you.
Not from this angle.
Not from moving forward.

. . . .

Parts of Opal People's rhythm were respectfully smuggled in from Track 1 on Tool's CD, Undertow, but the sheer intensity of it all was brought on by Track 3, Sober.

I wrote Opal People under the influence of speed on Christmas Day, 1998, my first Christmas alone. I am typing these notes on Christmas Day, 2000, my second Christmas alone. I am not on speed.

Opal People uses the term "bolt-action". I used the term again when I later wrote I Got Gone. When I perform Opal People and I Got Gone in the same night people tend to point out that the term "bolt-action" is used in both pieces. Thank you. Thank you, I know. Aside from Soul Coughing's use of word and line repetition I'm not a huge fan of that sorta thing. I am now going to abandon this paragraph.

Opal People is the result of two lives running quite parallel with one another and is nothing less than inspired by a light of my life, Danielle Plunkett.

Love is also opal
and silent
with water
she moves me.

OPAL PEOPLE [1998]

SHE TOLD ME IT WAS ALRIGHT TO EXPLODE AND BE FREE
BECAUSE SHE SAW THE PLEASURE REVOLVING ME
BECAUSE THAT'S MY KIND OF ENERGY
BECAUSE I'M AMAZING, SHE WAS SAYING, FOR THE THINGS I SEE
AND SHE'S PRETTY AMAZING TO ME

BUT I SAID,

"I WOULDN'T LOOK CEN-TERED
AND I WOULDN'T BE GROUN-DED
AND I MIGHT LOSE FO-CUS
WHEN THE PAST COMES TRYIN' TO STROKE US OFF
AND YOU MIGHT SEE THE MISTAKES I MAKE
BECAUSE I CAN'T DO ANYTHING
WITHOUT GETTIN' LOST IN IT
AND GOIN' FULL-CIRCLE BEFORE I STEP"

SEE THERE'S A VOICE THAT TAKES ME UNDER
AND SHE SEES THE WAY I NEED THE PAIN
SO WE GO INTO THE WORLD OF WONDER
BY THE SYSTEMATIC FLEE OF THESE TERRIFIED FEET
AND SHE STRIPS THOSE THOUGHTS AWAY
AND SOMETIMES, Y'ALL, THIS WON'T MAKE SENSE
BUT *SOMETIMES* AIN'T NO ACCIDENT

BECAUSE VISIONS DON'T DANCE ON THEIR OWN
SO SINCE WE'RE GONNA BE GOIN' SO FAR FROM HOME
WE'LL USE OUR WIDE EYES AND CAST OUR PLASTIC SEEDS
TO THOSE WHO LIKE TO PLAY HACKSAW JIGSAW
NAME-THAT-GREED

THEN WE'LL GO BOLT-ACTION
TO SICKLE THE STITCHES

AND STICK OUR STAINED GLASS FEET
INTO AN OPAL SKIN
WHERE WE'RE ALLOWED TO EXPLODE ALL OVER AGAIN
'CAUSE WHEN THE WATER AIN'T WRINKLED
WE DIVE RIGHT IN

AND YA KNOW WE BREATHE THAT WATER
WHEN IT'S COMIN' FROM DREAMS
WITH MOUNTAINOUS WAVES OF AMBER IN ITS GRAIN
THAT FLUTTERS LIKE HUMANS
REACHING FOR LIGHT
WHO'VE GOT 10,000 LBS OF SONGS IN THEIR EYES

AND WE NEVER DARE COME UP FOR AIR
IF WE'RE ONLY HALFWAY THROUGH

'CAUSE THEN WE WOULDN'T LOOK CEN-TERED
AND WE WOULDN'T BE GROUN- DED
AND WE MIGHT LACK *FOCUS*
AND I'M JUST COMIN' BACK TO TELL YA BEFORE THIS GETS
US OFF

SO IF YOU FINALLY MAKE IT
THERE'LL BE A GIANT RUSH OF RIVER
UNDER A GIANT VARNISH CLOUD
IT'LL BE WRAPPED IN GIANT STONES

AND *LOUD!*

LIKE SILENCE STANDING OUT

SO PLEASE

TAKE YER TIME

WITH

THE BUBBLE AND THE JET-BLANK STARE

AND REMEMBER WHAT IT TOOK TO GET HERE

BECAUSE IT WON'T BE PAST-TENSE, HALF-WIT SMOKE

IT'LL BE FLOW-INFLICTED OPAL DROVES

OF THOSE WHO KNOW HOW TO RISE AND GROW

AND HOW TO RESPOND TO THE END OF THE WORLD

"SO,"
SHE SAID,

"IT'S OKAY TO BE RA-CING
AND IT'S OKAY TO EX-PLODE
IF THAT'S WHAT IT'S GONNA TAKE FOR YOU TO FINALLY –

LET IT GO.

. . . .

Earlier in the book I said: My friend, Seth, gets incredibly flustered when there's a yearning in his heart that the tip of his tongue doesn't know how to translate. It makes him ball up inside like a fist. He wants to express himself so badly with words sometimes, but he doesn't always have the catalog of associations at hand to know which words deliver the appropriate expression without losing his cool.

My deadline for turning in this manuscript is tomorrow. I've put off writing an intro to A Waste for the very same reason Seth leaves a room in knots sometimes, like he wants to hug the ocean, but doesn't, because it's just so much. This poem deserves a proper introduction and — even though the stories of millions of suicides and murders, self-mutilators and children, lovers of life and healers will be left out — what I want you to know is this:

I tended bar at a place where the walls were painted black and the smoke rings made chains of clouds too thick to breathe sometimes, where old men with deep sadness in their eyes came to drink away the fact that they spent an entire lifetime either denying a paramount part of their own individual human experience, their sexuality. Many were beaten for it, ridiculed and hated because they did not desire intimacy the same way others wanted them to, despite the fact that each person feels desire inside them and can point to it on a map. The thing each of those drunk smokers wanted was to give and receive love the way their bodies and their hearts felt it. Not yours.

Beyond the convenient stereotypes and the easy dismiss of feminine cattiness, homosexual individuals are also so entirely human we give rise to healing and reason, and we do not necessarily feel the need for you to know about our sex lives until our respect, rights and choices are taken away based on them.

Although love is not an institution, those who choose to express love through the framework of legal marriage will no longer be denied. There are some they can't contain who know true equality does not encompass conditional freedom and — if we want to — we will marry.

I owe Ragan Fox many thanks for his chapbook Heterophobia. It opened doorways in my own approach and expression that I thought had been deleted by years of fear.

At the risk of overshadowing the impending poem, A Waste, I want you to read an important

. . . .

letter to George W. Bush, found as a Letter to the Editor in the March 5th, 2004 issue of Seattle Gay News:

Dear Mr. President,

I could not avoid you tonight as your support for a federal constitutional amendment banning same-sex marriage blared throughout the airport lounge via CNN. As I listened to your confusing messages about family and values and politics, I shared sadness with my fellow travelers about your continuing fear-driven approach to leadership. Your defense of traditional marriage rang hollow; rather, it was a poor endorsement for discrimination, ignorance and your conservative political base.

Uncharacteristically, I decided not to be angry, offended or cynical. Rather, I desperately want to understand you and your allies on this issue, and take the high road in that engagement. So I invite you, Laura and your daughters to spend a day with my family and explain why you are championing such a cause.

Spend a day with our energetic and cheerful seven-year-old son, Ben. Ben will treat you to an active day full of homework, piano lessons, Lego projects, friends, chores, soccer and baseball. Fully steeped in the values of love, sharing, friendship and learning, Ben is immensely proud of his two adoring and engaged parents, and wonderfully enriched by a diverse and supportive neighborhood.

Spend a day with our extraordinary community of friends and neighbors, who reflect the America of today and the future — mixed in race, language, background, family structures and ideas — but united in their deep commitment to our children, to creating a better future, to loving our country and to enjoying the richness of life.

Spend a day with our extended family that has supported us with unconditional love through good times and bad. Our parents, aunts, uncles, siblings, cousins, nieces and nephews spread around the country form the foundation of our world. Over the years we have celebrated countless joyous holidays and celebrations together, as well as helping them in endless ways through illnesses, financial problems, divorces and other family dramas.

Spend a day with us as we engage in our community as a family and as individuals, as we actively volunteer at Ben's school, as we have headed up the local United Way, and as we have worked tirelessly with many community organizations to improve the lives of our less-fortunate neighbors. Come join us as we sing and pray in church together.

Spend the day with me as the CEO of a fast-growing digital media company who understands the economic interests of supporting stable communities and families, who must

. . . .

include a vibrant 21st century inclusive workforce through rigorous recruiting and non-discriminatory practices, and who is forever seeking that elusive family-life-work balance.

Spend the day with us as we explain to our son, his friends and cousins, why the world can be a fragile place where people do bad things out of ignorance and fear, where people hate people for silly reasons, where leaders abuse power for political gain at the expense of innocent folks, and where people waste enormous emotion and energy on side issues when domestic and child abuse, poverty, racism, divorce and inadequate health care — the issues truly threatening the American family — go unattended.

Mr. President, please come spend a day with us. And then, over our evening family meal, after we have given our nightly thanks to our loving and hate-free God, explain to this same-sex household just what family values you are defending for the future of America.

Sincerely,
Steve Davis,
CEO of Corbis

A WASTE [2 0 0 3]

We'll call her "Sweet Angel."
Hugs herself when she's stupid.
Gets facials from a wonderful woman in the city who talks like a landslide.
Boys used to call her "Peach."
The way she said it still blurs me up like a massacre.
In an attempt to make me feel handsome, Sweet Angel said,
"If I was a girl your age and I found out you were gay
I'd just think, ya know, *what a waste*"

Okay, hey, Perky Cheeks,
if that was supposta be a compliment
please don't ever send me a care package.

A waste...
A waste is more like when I stole a woman's trust, love and virginity
then broke her heart
just to prove to the fellas that
I *REALLY* like fuckin' pussy.
That was a waste.

A waste were all the ceiling lights I broke juggling
steel
and cheek bones
gay
and Texas
glass ornaments
made of closets that can easily hang, hide and stretch
my dirty laundry on clotheslines
from San Mateo to Niagara Falls back to Texas
and you'll never see a thing.

Fourteen
and fading.

My Parents
on marriage # 8.

Me
keeping all of it
hidden
up in the air
like ducks in a row
ready to go down during huntin' season.

To some children
self-preservation and mirrors will always look
like a grown man with raw lips and lockjaw
whose hearts pounds out so fast for safety
it sounds like ice picks
chipping holes through the chest of a sculpture
his parents otherwise would have *loved* to show their friends.

A waste
were the years without light
or smile
or worth
the years I spent in places it's not fair for me to tell you about
like in the backs of adult arcades
where I learned that the only certainty some human beings will ever know
is this:

there's a naked
man

and there's a dark
room

everywhere.

These are children who will never be told

there is nothing wrong with being human
who are not allowed to love themselves
despite their crimes
who will have no one there to help them arrange
chaos in alphabetical order
once they realize that sometimes
being born
is really inappropriate.

They will be haunted by their ability to hate you
to give you back what they got from you.
It's the quickest slow death you'll never see
until the wind blows
on a quiet day
and you ain't got nobody there to hold.

Y'all, it is a waste
like the hundreds of gallons of gas I burned
pulling off into the alley so I could die
or scream
or clutch.
There will never be enough back road in this world
to make you understand
how much I loved him.

A waste is a nine-year-old boy
playing catch with the roof of his garage
who already understands that
his existence makes for the perfect insult —
GAY.
"You're so gay"
a.k.a. stupid
a.k.a. dumb
a.k.a. wrong mutherfucker
wrong wrong mutherfucker.
Do have any idea how gross it feels

to have to hide inside the pile of lies it takes
to make you, Sweet Angel,
Comfortable?

Knowing me
it's easy.
You can still twist your hair
and feel silly
look up the word tacky
and have a salad.
But when we're together
you pull bread apart with your fingers into bites sometimes so small
I gotta remind you, Peach:

It is okay

to be hungry.

*****

You're still fighting.
You're still grinding your teeth.
You're still not moving fast enough forward, but you're still after me.

You're still talking and talking, but you're still in over your head
because you still talk and talk by the gallon
but still don't wanna burn that padded bed.

And you still open wide for salt when it's pouring down your wounds.
And you still bow to gravity.
And you're still taking it literally.
And you're still laying down the law, but you still don't know the truth.

And you're still not sure what's happening here because you're still not gonna try.
And you're still addicted to way back when instead of coming back to life.

And I know ya don't wanna hear it
because ya still can't stand to see.
And I know you still won't drop your guard because I just might knock ya free.

Yeah but,
my point forever endlessly
is that you still don't know you're amazing.

You still don't know you're amazing.

You still don't know you're amazing for the things you see.

*****

A LITTLE DITTY CALLED HAPPINESS [1996]

That boy
sits on a log
eatin' pie
drinkin' fog
playin' fetch with a dog
that just won't run his way

and his girl
sits in a swing that don't sway
singin' songs about history
and wonders
Why's vanity look so good on me?

And Ma & Pa are callin' all
sayin', "Get on down to yer doctor's mall!"
He's got a special
on boobs
and lips
and butts
and cake

while Cousin's on the cellular phone
callin' more talk shows for the folks at home
who've got opinions on solutions for problems
that ain't their own
Ba ba bome bome   bome   bome

HA!

And let's hear it for the upper class
killin' Winnie-the-Pooh with the molds they cast
in this clash of titans that no longer remains in check
'cause Superman
broke his neck.

But there's a
a little ditty called Happiness
it says
I'm gonna walk away from this
before I lose my masterpiece
to an Etch-A-Sketch again.
and in the mornin' when I rise
if everybody's *really* being randomly kind
and if
I can feel as good as I do tonight -
then I'm gonna walk away from this
with a
a little ditty called Happiness.

But...

religion's paced the rats in this race
for a low fat succulent jumbo shake
while a man in the street
like an old pile of meat
buys groceries from the local aluminum can

and as they juggle his balls with tightened fists
in a world war on the streets of Wit
the "president" eats the smiles from our cheeks
puckers up and waves his hands.

And...

Ma & Pa they're callin' all
screamin', "Get on back to yer doctor's mall!"
He's got a special
on computer chips
for the brains
in our kids

while some drunk fool with a class at school
blows sawdust off his power tools
and looks down a row of the dummies
he's created
again.

But there's a
a little ditty called Happiness
it says
I'm gonna walk away from this
before I lose my masterpiece
to an Etch-A-Sketch again.
And in the mornin' when I rise
if they vacuum up the gun smoke out of the sky
if we can love ourselves despite the crimes
if we will drop our jaws at fire when it's flyin' out our eyes
and right now all come back to life and if
I can feel as good as I do tonight

then I'm gonna walk away from this
with a
a little ditty called Happiness.

BIOGRAPHY

BUDDY WAKEFIELD is the two-time Individual World Poetry Slam Champion featured on NPR, the BBC, HBO's Def Poetry Jam, and most recently signed to Strange Famous Records. In 2004 he won the Individual World Poetry Slam Finals thanks to the support of anthropologist and producer Norman Lear then successfully defended that title at the International Poetry Festival in Rotterdam, Netherlands against the national champions of seven European countries with works translated into Dutch.

In 2005 he won the Individual World Poetry Slam Championship title again and has gone on to share the stage with nearly every notable performance poet in the world including Saul Williams, Sage Francis, Alix Olson, Derrick Brown and Utah Phillips in hundreds of venues internationally from Comedy Central's Hudson Theater and Scotland's Oran Moore to San Quentin State Penitentiary, House of Blues (New Orleans) and CBGB's.

In the spring of 2001 Buddy left his position as the executive assistant at a biomedical firm in Gig Harbor, WA, sold or gave away all he owned, moved to the small town of Honda Civic and set out to live for a living, touring every major poetry venue in North America through 2003. He still tours full time while co-managing The Bullhorn Collective (a talent agency founded by Wakefield, made up of 30+ of the most accomplished performance poets alive), and considers his recent tours with Ani DiFranco the highlight of his career thus far.

Born in Shreveport, LA, mostly raised in Baytown, TX, now claiming Seattle, WA as home, Buddy has been a busker in Amsterdam, a lumberjack in Norway, a street vendor in Spain, a team leader in Singapore, a re-delivery boy, a candy maker, a street sweeper, a bartender, a maid, a construction worker, manager of a CD store, a bull rider and a booking agent. Wakefield is a growth junkie, an expert witness to the moon, avid player of marbles in the trees, elated son of a guitar repair woman, wingman of Giant Saint Everything, is void of S.T.D.'s, and remains generally hopeful for his health despite an abusive relationship with free range pastry buffets.

Buddy, a Board of Directors member with Youth Speaks Seattle and member of Team Seattle 2006 and 2007 for the National Poetry Slam Finals is honored that his work is published internationally and has been used to win national collegiate forensics competitions. Also a member of Solomon Sparrow's Electric Whale Revival, Buddy is known for delivering raw, rounded, high vibration performances of humor and heart.

ACKNOWLEDGMENTS

I hesitate to recognize just a handful of folks only because there are dozens more I will fail to mention who spent valued energy making sure I survived the two year and four month tour right through to this moment. There is a very long list of those who gave their homes and time and love and I am endlessly thankful. After perusing a 400-date tour page to jog my memory regarding those I need to thank at this point, I see that I can only open-endedly give thanks to a few for the sake of focus. This book is for those performance poets who — in their own special way — delivered different versions of hope directly to my heart when no one else was lookin': Rachel Kann, Sage Francis, Corbet Dean, Cheryl Maddalena, Lucky Dave, Daled & Naz, Mike McGee, Marc Bamuthi Joseph, Eitan Kadosh, The Suicide Kings, Dan Stevens, Paradox, R.C. Weslowski, Seth Jarvis, Ben Trigg and Steve Ramirez, Jeremy Richards, Raegan Truax, Shihan VanClief, Cynthia French, Vadim Litvak, Karrie Waarala...

This book is for Lucy Anderton who reminded me that I am a survivor, and that I am really good at surviving, but that eventually I have to stop practicing survival in order to be great at living.

This book is for every touring poet who's endured more humiliating venues than *Hedwig and the Angry Inch* can shake a stick at.

This book is dedicated to a small number of individuals and groups whom I don't necessarily have the honor of keeping mutual company with, but who have inspired me deeply and lifted me higher into this human experience: Teatro ZinZanni, Saul Williams, Blackalicious, Mike Doughty, Cirque Du Soleil (I'm not puttin' the stupid TM sign after that), Michael Moore, The Polyphonic Spree, Benjamin Hoff, Ween and Speed Lovich.

Many of the performance poets who inspired me to be in the blessed position of writing these very words — like Tim Sanders and Annie

LaGanga — will not be known for their undeniably profound influence in the realm of Poetry Slam/performance poetry/spoken word, but I thank them forever as they move on to other avenues for driving their own dreams through to fruition. This book is for them.

This book is for my closest friends outside of the poetry community who have sheltered me with a wealth of knowledge, and have at times given up excessive amounts of personal space so I could accomplish my tiny dreams: Jon and Sherri Berardi, Shona Strauser and Wileen Maniago, Danielle Plunkett and Tim Johnson, Benjamin Morse, Jeremy and Shana Shouldis, Shane Kuhlberg, Seth Terrell, Danny Sizemore, Tiffany Hill, Lace Williams, Joe and Stephen, and my badass mom.

This book is dedicated to the logistical foundation of Poetry Slam, those who pitched this circus tent and have provided the priceless medium. There are hundreds of essential players, especially the folks at Poetry Slam, Inc., but I wish mostly to thank Gabrielle Bouliane for her commitment and loyalty. Without her I would be catatonic.

To Amanda Johnson for letting me steal the comparison of Wife Swap and The Bachelor to the sanctity of marriage.

To Chris Owen and Sharon Sensor for the backpack and D'Arcy the Guitar, so I could keep movin' after Memphis kicked me in the crack.

This thing is for the first time I saw the light, when there were three — thank you A.J. & Dogger.

To Lane Stroud for editing this three years later and for sneering a little when I lifted 'growth junkie' off her tongue; without the challenge, I couldn't have taken the name.

And for all those moments with all those individuals in all those random places who've shared in and supported my journey, and who — most of all — made me laugh...

...and I remember seein'm break and run off by themselves
and I remember they were full force in song throwing their bodies
around like wands
and I remember, clearly, they wanted out.

...and I remember when the train came they all hopped it
though they never claimed to ride that way
but it was midnight
and it was goin' to Georgia
and it was free.

release

Printed in the United States
204751BV00001B/1-105/A